The Widow's Garment

Cheryl Singletary

Copyright © 2012 Cheryl Singletary

All rights reserved.

ISBN:13: 9780972667500
ISBN-10:0972667504

DEDICATION

In Loving memory of Stephen, Connie and Daddy, your lives here have enriched my life and inspired me to write.
Mama and Debbie, your strength and endurance changed my life. I will never be the same.

CONTENTS

Acknowledgments/Dedications

Preface

Introduction by Dr. Lafayette Scales

1. A Time to Die
2. A Time to Laugh/A Time to Cry
3. A Time to Mourn
4. A Time to Grieve
5. A Time to Heal

Prologue

ACKNOWLEDGMENTS

Special thanks to:
My Lord and Savior Jesus Christ!
My loving husband: Nathaniel Singletary, your undying support anchors my soul. My beautiful children and grandchildren: Cierra, Dexter, Nat, Deja, Joshua, Emaari, Jillisa Quinn, D'ajah, David and Lillie. My Family: Walkers and Singletarys. All of my midwives, intercessors and pushers.
My daughter; Deja Watson-Chandler for articulating and designing the cover.
My Pastor and Co Pastor: Jamie and Tanya Croone, Redeeming Love Christian Church. All my friends and love ones.

INTRODUCTION BY DR. LAFAYETTE SCALES

There are many times and seasons in life. Life offers many contradictions and paradoxes. There are many conditions that come on us that we do not ask for or initiate. When they come, there are many responses we can have. We can adjust and keep our eyes on our goal and vision, keep moving, or we can stop, cave in, and quit. Life has its joys and sorrows. Life has pleasures and pains. Life has its celebrations and its distresses.

There is no pain and discomfort that distresses the soul of a person like that of an unexpected death of a spouse. Sudden death knocks the wind out of us. The hurt is so deep medicine can't numb it. Friends cannot soothe it. Encouraging words do not touch it. Normal daily life does not ease it. The soreness and suffering is so difficult, at times words cannot express them. Tears and sighs become our language, prayer, and worship. Yet the heartbreak and agony get us acquainted with something inside us we were not familiar with. We discovered a God who knows and understands our sorrow, loss, grief, and sadness. He is there to help us through. He is there to help us know Him in our misery.

The Widow's Garment reaches out to everyone who has ever experienced loss. The Widow's Garment reaches out to everyone who is going through the agony of grief. This real-life account will comfort and strengthen those who may be in the crisis of pain and grief. The message bodily, honestly, and bravely conveys there is hope, help, and assistance from the Lord. Whatever pain does not kill you will help make you.

Permit the Spirit of God to soothe, strengthen, and aid you as you walk with Cheryl Singletary through a death and resurrection experience of life. Receive the comfort of the Holy Spirit. Receive a new perspective from the Holy Spirit. Let the Holy Spirit breathe new life as you pursue Him and find Him through The Widow's Garment.

PREFACE

Walk with me through the pages of tragedy, restoration, and final justification of a new life in Christ. I am writing this book as an open epistle to those who have experienced the loss of a loved one. I am recounting the experience of my life through the design of the Holy Spirit. The word tells us to "comfort those with what you have been comforted." My prayers are that as you walk with me through this tragedy, you will see the healing hand of God, the hope of God through Christ, and his ability to make all things new.

In this life, we will wear many garments. Our garments display what season we are in. Our garments change as season's change, and as seasons change so do our lives. Solomon spoke the great words, "To everything there is a season..." I am writing on particular seasons is my life and the garment that I wore by the intricate, delicate design of destiny. A garment with which Jesus entrusted me. A garment so precious that he tenderly put it upon my life from the closet of the cross, that I could experience His glorious resurrection power.

THE CHANGING OF THE GARMENT

PROVERBS 31:25 (AMP)

Strength and dignity are her clothing and her position is strong and secure: she rejoices over the future [the latter day of time to come, knowing that she and her family are in readiness for it!

In a vision, I saw myself with a beautiful sapphire-sequined evening gown walking with my head lifted high. My countenance was brighter than the sequins on the gown, and as I was walking, a great hand came and violently ripped my dress into two pieces, the other hand held a gown of sackcloth. The hand gestures with question, "Will you wear this tonight instead?"

What was wrong with what I was wearing? It fit perfectly. It was so beautiful and brilliant. What was wrong? Not to mention that the alternate garment was so ugly. The hand gently offered the dress of ashes and sackcloth asking the questions of my predestined (foretold) future. *Will you wear the garment I have made for you?*

Still, in another vision I saw a tree stump that had stood alone. Then with tremendous force the great hand came and split the stump in half with an ax, revealing a ground of deep dark fertile rich soil. Up from the soil I saw a crisp green plant emerge, so green that it's color dripped with life. The plant grew and grew into a bountiful tree. In myself, I thought the tree would bear ripened fruit, but instead they were transparent crystal diamond like jewels hanging where there would be fruit. I gazed upon the tree in wonderment, tears streaming down my face I heard God ask yet another question that shook the earth I stood upon, "What will you give for this tree?"

Both were visions that remain with me to this day. Through intense worship and struggles of flesh, I answered the voice of my vision. "Yes, I will wear your garment Lord, and I will give my life for Your rich, transparent will to be done in my life."

You see, our life as we know it is the stump that stands useless without true life. The Master destroys what was, so His purpose is revealed. Through time, He plants His truth in our will and the fruit of His brokenness is transparent shining stones of truth wherein we fulfill our destiny in Him.

The sequined dress was the life that I made myself. The life that I walked in, my will, my way, my truth, up until that time. That life was good. I served the Lord. I loved Him and I loved the life I was living. But the higher calling required new apparel. It was time for my garment to be charged. God has beckoned me to dance with Him with outstretched hands. He lured me with His charming grace, and wooed me as He kept saying, "What will you give to wear this garment while we dance?" Do you want to know me in the power of my resurrection? Do you really want to fellowship in my suffering? Will you be made comfortable with my death? Will you change garment tonight, Cheryl?"

The gown of my choice was good for the inner court, but the higher place required a garment of sackcloth and ashes. I could not move in the jeweled gown of the inner court. The innermost court calls for you to partake of the transparent crystal stone of truth. He is the tree of life. As we eat of Him, He establishes truth in the inward part. In the innermost court, you are stripped from your glory and changed into His glory. We are naked in the innermost court. I found that in the lure of knowing Him and being made conformable unto His death, the garment is humility. It bears no jewels. Its attention is turned away from you. You are not only stripped by fellowshipping in the suffering of Christ, but you are conformed in the humility of His death. Humility has no reputation, no glory of its own. It's covering is irritable, like sackcloth, never giving room for comfort, stagnate or lukewarm. You learn the truth of Christ and the wisdom of Christ humility.

I finally accepted the garment my Lord made for that season in my life. I was already stripped through the pain of His plan and strategy for me. I remembered being accused of not accepting my husband's death; accused of pressuring my dear beloved to the threshold of death with my childish demands of love. Fingers pointed telling me how to grieve, some saying "cry", others saying, "don't." Some told me to laugh while others said I was too happy. I felt as if I was losing my mind. But...

Humanity stood up in my behalf as I found myself praying for those who didn't know the demise of their wicked tongues. God used their tongues as the tool to slash away and strip who I was, constantly keeping me on my face crying purging tears. He cleansed away condemned cities and old buildings of the past, tore off the old and brought me forth into the new.

During this season, the enemy sought to take my life. He came to steal my character, kill my integrity, and destroy my mind. However, through the testing of faith and obeying God not to retaliate to the accusations, I humbled myself under his mighty hand. His integrity and a renewed mind suddenly emerged from the pains of death. I was a better person, and did not become bitter. I changed my garments. I put on the dress that His kind hand offered me and it fit me perfectly.

CHAPTER 1:
A TIME TO DIE

We live this life with an expected end... We learn death is an inevitable part of life.

I WANT TO LIVE....

As I reflect upon that day, what I remember most was the rush. Never really taking a lot of time for anything, I was always busy. Busy working, busy singing, busy taking care of the kids, busy taking care of my "man."

This time I was rushing from the beauty shop to church. "I can't be late; my worship team is singing. Where is he?" Then he pulled up. The most handsome man I've ever seen, smiling at me and making the rush quiet down. With just one look, I felt like a baby rocking back and forth in the arms of its mother, peaceful and secure. His voice was like the hush of the break of dawn.

He reaches over to kiss me and says, "Hello, sweetheart. Do you have everything?"

"Yes, but we have to hurry baby." "I know," he replied. "Get in."

Did I tell you his smile lit up the whole atmosphere? And to think he was my husband.

We talked about what happened that day and I could see concern in his eyes. His sister had called and asked if we would take custody of her children in the event of her death.

He said, "What an awesome responsibility." He felt she dwelt too much on preparing for death or negative things.

"I want to live!"

His words echoed in the atmosphere and startled me for a second. When I looked in his eyes, the sincerity and zest for the positive in life mirrored in my eyes, "I want to live and I want the best for you and the kids. We need to start planning now. We need to start investigating and using wisdom in our time and money". "Do you know how much God has in store for us?"

All throughout service that night, I could not help but think about our conversation and destiny. I cannot explain the feeling I had but my heart was beating fast with excitement and expectation of the new direction we were going in our endeavors for a better, even fuller life.

After a long ride home from church service we pulled into the garage. We were both tired and spent from the day, and I didn't want to sit in the car and talk like we sometimes did. I wanted to put the kids to bed and lay in his lap. As I put my hand on the door handle to go inside the house he said, "I'm so honored to have you as my wife. You are so beautiful tonight." I turned to tease him expecting eyes full of desire, but what I saw was eyes full of love and admiration. He starred for a long moment in my eyes and said, "I love you, Cheryl Denise." I smiled. My heart felt as though I was dreaming. How could this love be so real after eighteen years of relationship?

That was the last time I heard those words from my husband.

Sometimes what we wish were a dream is actually reality, and what we wish were reality is only a dream.

We went into the house and put the kids to bed and prepared for "our time." You know, the husband and wife time, the time without the kids, for our intimacy or for our sanity or whatever we needed for us.

"Come here, baby," I said as I went downstairs. He replied with a pat on my behind, "I'm hungry. I'm going to fix me something to eat." I went downstairs. My twenty-one-month-old son, Emaari followed saying, "I want Mommy."

As I rocked Emaari to sleep, I watched my husband enjoy his special meal, one peanut butter and jelly sandwich, one bologna sandwich, Fritos and strawberry Kool-Aid with lots of ice. He was content. "Aren't you gonna sit next to me baby?" I asked. He winked. "I'll be right over", he said, knowing full well I would be asleep very soon, and he could possibly catch the rest of the basketball game on TV or play his bass guitar (one of his favorite things to do).

The next chain of events are very vivid and replay in slow-motion when I recall them in my mind's eye. I was awakened by a loud sound. I cannot remember if it was my husband's voice, the crash of his body from a fall, or a loud clatter.

I woke up and looked at the TV. It was off. I ran into the next room and my husband lay there on his back rocking back and forth, in a great amount pain. "Can you move?" I said. He could not make a sound. His face was extremely red and stricken with agony. It's going to be all right baby. "Hold on, I'm here baby." I called 911 and began to talk still unclear if he had been shot, electrocuted, or had fallen and hit his head; all I knew was he was hurt.

The operator asked if he was still breathing. By this time he was breathing through clenched teeth. Each breath was very labored and antagonizing. His color was changing and every time I touched him, he would try harder to breathe.

I begin CPR. Although my husband was stout man, 6 feet and 225 pounds, he seemed even larger while he lay there on the floor. His helpless body overwhelmed me.

The police arrived first, "Is your husband armed?" I could not understand the question. I responded, "Armed? No, he is dying! He is downstairs." The paramedics were soon to follow and they begin their duties of fighting for my husband's life.

I put my son in the bed and I remember the look in his eyes, very scared, very fragile. "You have to go to sleep baby." I kissed him, closed his eyes, and said a small prayer, "In the name of Jesus". He went to sleep. I started down the stairs and watch them work husband. With all my insight in the word of God and my knowledge as a warrior in Christ, all I could do was say, "Jesus." No tremendous words, no scriptural text or reference just "Jesus"!

I heard the clap of the life paddles as they jolted Steve's body. As he lay there, my mind drifted to one of the happiest days of my life.

"Cheryl, where do you want to go tonight?"

Friday night was our night out. We had discussed marriage previously so I thought he purchased my engagement ring. Every Friday, I would look as pretty as possible and rehearse how he would propose to me and how I would say, "Maybe", or "Let me sleep on it and I will get back with you."

We both were practical jokers. We loved to laugh. Anyways, each Friday I will leave frustrated. This had gone all summer and it was now November and still, no ring. Every time I would casually ask about the ring, he would reply sarcastically like "good things come to those who wait, "What ring?" or just change the subject completely.

He picked me up that night looking as handsome as usual. He was wearing a white shirt, which complimented his dark features, black baggy pants, which were popular for the 80s and his gleaming white "Pepsodent" smile dazzled me. As he opened the door for me he said "Hey there Angel, you look beautiful. Right Steve, you always say that. "Well, he interjected, you shouldn't be so beautiful."

"Let's hurry, because I want to spend some time with Sandy tonight. " I said and I rushed through dinner even though he tried to prolong it. I' d joke. He tried to be serious. Finally, he said, "Let's go baby", resigned and seemingly frustrated.

On the way home, he held my hand and said, "You want to go on a walk?"

"Steve, it's cold outside". I said. He pleaded with me and assured me it will be a short one.

We stopped at Confluence Park, a park right in the center of Columbus, Ohio, on the riverfront with luminous lights surrounding a beautiful fountain. There, children would throw coins and make wishes and couples would hold hands and romance each other. The fountain was lovely in the evening with colored lights that bounced of the coins in the water and danced with the moonlight on the sidewalk. He stopped in the front of the water. The moon reflecting his athletic silhouette as he skipped a rock nervously across the water. I stood shivering from the cold.

"Cheryl, do you love me as much as I love you?" I started to say something funny, but he reached in his pocket and brought out a tissue. "Steve, yes, of course I love you. Don't cry." He put the tissue on the ground and put his knee upon it and said, "Cheryl Denise Walker, will you be my wife?"
 Yes, I will. I screamed. We hugged and he danced around saying, "She said yes!" We got in the car and he began blowing the horn, driving downtown in the middle of the night shouting, "She said yes!"

 Those horns rang in my head and somehow brought me into the present clatter of the paramedics bringing down the stretcher.

"Jesus," I whispered. I thought I needed prayers going up from my friends because my husband is fighting for his life. I called my dearest friends: Connie, Darryl, Gary, Tosca, Marcia, Linda, Roshawn and Terissa. Darryl came over immediately to stay with the kids, who still miraculously remained sleep throughout all the commotion.

 I prepared for the ride to the hospital.

As I was getting dressed, I thought about the words God had given me, "Are you ready for revival? Are you ready for the utter, shaking, and uprooting of everything, so that which is unshakable will remain. Will you endure?"

That's it. That's is it Lord! (not knowing fully the drastic traumatic changes that were about to unfold). This is the shaking?!

I began to intercede and pray in the Spirit. I went downstairs. Tosca and Gary had arrived. I glanced at my husband with

I.V. tubes in him. I was very afraid to see him in such a fragile state. I felt helpless and unsure.

"Should I ride in the ambulance?" I asked the paramedics. "How is he doing?"

He replied, "You probably should ride with someone else, but that would be your decision." The look in his eyes told me that Steve's condition was fatal.

In the car with Gary and Tosca, I told them to call down heaven and pray only in the spirit. "You take your hands off of him Satan! You will not have my husband. He is a man full of destiny. A man of valor. He has three children to raise and you must take your hands off of him, in the name of Jesus!"

In the midst of my praying, just as plain as day, I heard the Lord say, "It is Me Cheryl." "What Lord?" "It is I," says the Lord.

With these words came a hush in my spirit. I told them to stop warring because God said it was Him. He was doing something and we should allow His sovereignty to prevail.

There was silence for the longest (10 minute) ride to the hospital. When we arrived some of my family and friends from church where they waiting. I do not know how word got around so fast, but it did.

I went inside and asked how my husband was doing. The paramedics said, "Things look bleak."

"Bleak," I said as I turned in walked through the doors of the hospital. "I need to be by myself and hear from the Lord."

I walked around the parking lot with an unexplained numbness in my soul, yet I was keenly aware in my spirit. I began talking to the Lord. "Lord, what are you doing?"

He said, "Cheryl, do you trust me?" I said, "God what do you mean?" Again, "Do you trust me?" "Lord are you going to take my husband?" He said, "Do you trust me? "Yes, Lord. I have nowhere else to turn."

It was then that Gary came to me and said the doctor wanted to see me. They led me into the room where we had received the tragic news of my father's death three months earlier. A room where I had already become familiar. I am sure my friends did not know the room's purpose. Their eyes were full of questions, hope, and concern.

We waited there without words until the screech of the door made us focus our undivided attention on the person entering. The nurse looked at me with pity and asked, "Mrs. Watson, was your husband sick or on any medication?"

"Was my husband?" I guess the keyword being, WAS. I answered with all impatience of the world and demanded "Is my husband dead?" "Yes, Mrs. Watson." I had a feeling of unbelief, yet somehow, I knew it was true.

Utter despair overtook me. I felt like I was alone in a capsule. I could see no one, feel anyone, or hear anyone.

Somehow, I picked up the phone and calmly called my mother to share the news.

"Mama, he's dead." I let the phone drop to her agonizing sobs of "No Cheryl, it can't be, it can't be!"

Suddenly, I was aware of the people and the pain in the room. I found myself in the arms of Tosca and Gary. I wanted to talk to Steve one last time. "Take me to where he is, "I said. In a daze, we walked to his room.

I cannot explain the atmosphere, but it felt as through the presence of my husband's spirit was there hovering over his lifeless body. I laid my head on his mountainous chest and began to tell him it was okay. I knew how much he loved the kids and I. I also knew that if he had a choice between eternity and this life, he would have chosen eternity. I shared some intimate words that only he would understand and held him until his body was no longer warm with life. I kissed his forehead, wiped his mouth of the fluid that evidenced his last struggle of war in his flesh upon this earth. "I love you baby, I always will."

Sometimes what we wish were dreams, is actually reality.

THOUGH YOU SLAY ME

I went out the door of Steve's hospital room into a realm that is unexplainable to me even to this day. All I know is that when I walked out the door I was caught up in a very pillowed comfort zone called peace. The God of Comfort touched me with His compassionate hands and set me in a place called his bosom.

Leaving the hospital, I was greeted by my mother-in-law. "How is he?" I could barely control myself, but managed to say "Mom, he's gone. "As I walked away I heard her cry, "No Cheryl, he's not....

I sat down on the curb at the back of the hospital parking lot and my pastor, Lafayette Scales, joined me.

 Lafayette has always been a levelheaded man of God, full of integrity and strength. But that night, I saw only the compassion of humanity in his face. I asked him, "Why did this happen?" He said, "I don't know." He did not try to muster up any words or excuses just ..."I don't know." When he said those words, his humanity embraced me more than his arms.

I cried, "Just give me a word from God to stand on."

He said, "Trust in the Lord with all your heart and lean not to your own understanding."

Then he sat down and began to talk. You see, Steve had just left his job to go to school. He sent me to school three years previously. We did not have insurance and weren't prepared for such a tragedy. We felt we had time. We were young and foolish.

Lafayette told me not to worry about a thing, "We will take care of you." Then shared his experience of losing his father. We talked until we both felt we could face what was ahead.

Lafayette always makes you feel that he is a touchable man of God, not far away from issues of life. But that night, I saw him from a different light. We were both looking unto our Heavenly Father with fragile hearts, depending upon that same God, and trusting Him to carry us through. Since that night I have called him my brother.

"Are you ready to go inside," he asked. I nodded and let out a big sigh.

Lafayette gave me what the words of his sermon only whisper, the ability to feel the natural pain that Christians sometime hide through masked faces. The truth is in this world we will have tribulations and suffer loss. However, we can grasp the hand of Christ who strengthens us. His strength carries our weakened vessels of flesh upon His beaten back, we overcome because He overcame, we endure because He endured. We fellowship in His sufferings when we ask to know Him.

As we walked back into the crowd of outstretch arms of what seemed like a million people, every step, every breath, even the sound of my clothes rustling while I walked, was intensified in amplified in my ears. It was as if each part of my being separated- my soul was spent and wounded as if it had taken a bullet to the heart, my body was tired and aching to be held by my beloved; but my spirit was somehow full of peaceful determination. I wanted to run away into another dimension, but my spirit stood in strength.

I got past the hugs and tears and managed to sit in a chair alone in the next room.

As they all gathered to pray and I found myself saying to the Lord, "Through you slay me, yet I will serve you," while a silent tear ran down my cheek, dropping softly onto my heart.

CHAPTER 2:
A TIME TO LAUGH, A TIME TO CRY, A TIME TO EMBRACE

Grieving has many faces, it is difficult to name them. Each face reflects the soul's pain, causing us to emotionally respond......

FAMILY TO RESCUE

As I stood at the hospital desk signing papers, my eyes met with my sister, Mari. I knew then that I was not dreaming and everything went black. Sorrow reserved in the depths of grief rushed from the place it had been hiding. Mari picked me up and rocked me back and forth saying "It's alright Cheryl... shhhh. I'm here now."

Through the tears I managed to tell her that Steve was where his heart longed to be and he was happy.

Steve would say words like, "I can't wait to see Heaven, to hear and play unspoken notes of angelic music, to have unlimited time in the presence of the Father."

He really loved the Lord. He was the sincerest man of God you could meet. He loved me, he adored he kids, but if he was ever given the choice to be here on earth or with Jesus, he would bluntly say, "I'm outta here, see ya!"

She continued to listen to my words with compassion and comforted me with her love.

My brother Roy bought my mom to the hospital. Although she was recovering from surgery and could barely walk, she wanted to make sure I was okay. I remember the look on my brother's face, searching my eyes to see if we were dreaming. Searching for me to make him laugh as before, but also trying to be strong. I walked to the car to mama and hugged her tight. Her comforting arms hushed my tears. "Shhhh.... baby it's alright, he's with the Lord now shhh........"

My family has always sheltered me, always tried to keep me from the pains of life, struggles, and poverty that has passed through generations. But that night there was no one to fix the broken vase, no one to take my punishment, no one to fight for me. Nothing could bring my husband back. I was the "baby" of the family and no one wanted to see me endure such tragedy.

However, tragedy separates hands and hearts and limits the reach of flesh. No one could rescue me from this pain that I had to endure.

Mari said, "Let's go home." That idea seemed to be the right one.

WHAT SHALL I DO?

The worst feeling in the whole wide world is the thought of bringing pain of any sort to your children. I remember wishing I could bear all the pain. I remember that the feeling of inadequacy, of not being able to rescue them was almost unbearable. I kept saying, "Oh God, how can I do this? What can I say?"

Their relationship was so close to their father. He would always fix what needed to be repaired, from broken toys to broken hearts. Together they would have pillow fights, make noise, read and create their own stories. He spent a lot of time with them because he loved them very much. They meant so much to him.

What do you say? How do you tell your children that the most significant man in their lives, our secure foundation, was gone? How do you tell a child that their father is gone and he will not be back in this life?

My heart hurt so much, the lump in my throat was so big, I could not breathe, So I prayed. I prayed from my gut with an intensity that is beyond the realm of this world.

God answered with "Time." He gave me "time" to gather myself and time to breathe. Although it was only a few hours, it was time. That time gave me wisdom and strength to gather myself and trust the articulation of the Holy Spirit.

When I walked through the door I thought I would collapse. I felt dizzy and the atmosphere was like the darkness when you shut your eyes tight. It was like shadowed square images of psychedelic dots exploding into firecrackers that invaded my sense of being, I was overwhelmed. It was unbelievable, like seeing through closed eyes blind to reality.

I managed to look to the ground. Tears came to my eyes when I saw the remains of what was once called clothing that had been violently cut away from Steve's body.

I wanted to lie down, but where? There were many rooms in my house that I wanted to avoid because of the ordeal, such as the basement and the dining room. I went straight to my children's rooms. They were asleep. The thought of entering my room nauseated me. So, I stood in my son's room and starred out the window. I could hear my family entering the door downstairs. They all came upstairs where I was.

The support of each of my family members brought a great deal of comfort. Not with words, but with their presence and genuine concern massaging the excruciating pain that my heart felt.

I remember my niece, Dawnesa entering the room. She was Steve and I's first love. We loved her as if she was our own daughter. I could see her struggling to avoid eye contact. She had that "I've done something wrong look." I asked her to come sit beside me. I held her tight. She said "Aunt

Cheryl, I didn't get to tell him I love him. I told him to leave my house when you guys came over last night. I didn't even say good-bye."

"It's okay baby," and I began to rock her softly in a rhythm answered by the sobs of her broken heart. Suddenly, she felt like a child again in my arms.

We begin reminiscing on good memories of Steve. She said, "Remember when I woke up from a bad dream and Steve came to the rescue. He came crashing through my door, kicking karate kicks and hiding like a secret agent, turning the corner cautiously as if he was in a movie." "Yeah," I said. We broke into hysterical laughter and then cried. We really didn't know if we should laugh or cry, so we did both. We talked for hours remembering all we could about our lives with Steve. My sisters came in to the room and shared their stories too. We held each other while sitting on the floor, finding comfort in our words. I looked outside the window and saw the dawn break.

THE GIFTS

"Where's Daddy?" My eldest daughter, Cierra, who was eight years old at the time, had awakened from her sleep and entered into the room. Suddenly my heart was in my throat. "C'mere baby." I led her into the bathroom and sat her on my lap. I held her close and told her I loved her. Cierra was a laid-back child, very seldom displaying any real emotion. Although she enjoyed hugs, she really did not go for mush and gush.

"Baby, remember Grandpa being sick in the hospital and he died?" "Yes," she replied. "Well, Daddy got sick last night and he went to the heaven with Grandpa." She jerked away and looked at me with utter bewilderment. "What happened to him," she asked with big tears rimming her eyes. I felt like running or hitting a wall... anything not to see the hurt I saw in her eyes. It cut me like a blunt knife ripping everything in jagged pieces.

I held her and asked the Holy Spirit to talk through me. I took her face and held it in my hands and told her that although her daddy was in heaven and she could never touch him again, she could close her eyes and he would always be in my heart. "Can't you feel him Cierra," I said, fighting back the screams inside me. "Can't you feel him there, baby?" I squeezed her close enough to listen to my heart. "Every time you need to feel your daddy, please come and find him right here baby."

We cried and clung to each other for our literal lives. We needed to know that we were alive and not going anywhere. We had suffered a great loss and in that moment, all we had left of our beloved was each other. She needed to feel me and I needed to feel her finding comfort in the Steve she had in her, and while she found comfort in the Steve inside of me. She gave me the strength of her name, Cierra, which means mountainous.

She let go and left the bathroom with dazed eyes, finding shelter in the bedroom with my family. One down, two to go, I thought, and I was not looking forward to it. I stayed in the bathroom with my head in my hands, silently praying that I would wake up from this nightmare, and with that thought, Deja, my four-year-old child, walked into the bathroom.

I told her the same words that I told Cierra, but she didn't respond with words. She simply sobbed with the pain that only death can bring, and I knew she somehow understood the pain. Deja always amazed me with her wisdom of discernment of the atmosphere. She has the ministry of comfort. Her name means "refreshing, a new day, remembrance." She looked at me through her tears, saying "Don't cry mommy, we will see him again." She then kissed me and went away... leaving the refreshing of her name and the comfort that comes in her bright colorful package.

My two-year-old son, Emaari, and Steve were inseparable. From the time Emaari's gender was known, Steve would talk to his "warrior" son. He would talk to my belly and tell him how much fun they were going to have playing football and how big Emaari's train track was going to be, and how they were not going to let us, girls, play with them. He entered the world in his dad's arms, holding his fists straight out just like superman.

Steve was proud of his son and although he cherished his daughters, he found security in his son. When Emaari entered the bathroom, he said "The police took my daddy?" He had seen the police come in and saw the rush of the paramedics before I put him to bed. I am not sure what or how much he saw, but I believe God allowed him to see his father exit this life to experience a great lesson. Emaari saw his dad fight like a warrior to live. I strongly believe that the impartation of strength was exchanged while Emaari looked at his dad entering eternity, just like his father watched him enter into this life. The exchange was powerful and evident in my son's behavior.

I held Emaari's hands. They are a Watson trademark. Strong enough to carry heavy loads yet soft enough to caress the fragile. I kissed those hands begotten from his father. I said, "No son, the police didn't take your daddy, Jesus took your daddy with him." "Is he coming back," he asked. "Yes, when Jesus returns, Daddy will come back with Him," I replied. Then he went downstairs to see if Jesus and his daddy had returned.

Emaari gave me hope in his determined, warm, childlike faith. He still waits for the return of Jesus and his hero, his dad.

My children come to me often for gifts and rewards. Sometimes just for support and love. However, that day I found the precious gift that lay in each of them. Cierra gave me strength. Deja gave me comfort. Emaari gave me hope. Those gifts gave me life.

After telling the children the tragic news, I followed Emaari down the steps and sat down exhausted, tired of feeling so alone. I looked outside and Joseph, a family friend, was on his knees praying and crying on my lawn at the crack of dawn.

Then they came, all of them with something special to give me. Some gave a word from God, some a warm hug, some gave a loving look, and some a cheering smile.

They came bearing food, money, and cards. Some came to clean, some came to cook, some came to baby-sit. They came to support the children and I. They brought all they had to the table of comfort. Visitors came frequently, some with words of encouragement, while others brought pity. It was so overwhelming that my family decided to escort me to what I fondly remember as the "upper room," my bedroom. No one could enter without passing security guards (Michelle, Tosca, and Mari).

I spent Thursday, April 28th through Friday, April 29th in the upper room. Most of the time I was in a daze, fading in and out. Some things I remember clearly... being rocked in the arms of my dear spiritual mother while she serenaded me with "Yes Jesus Loves a Me;" Steve's closet friends holding me tight, vowing their support to the children and I, the couples in the church imparting strength and comfort; the men of the church sitting around my room talking about Steve from a man's perspective. They agreed on two things unanimously - he loved God with all of his heart and he loved his children and I. Those things he openly displayed through the life he lived.

There was a select nucleus of friends that came beside me and walked in places I literally could not. They made all the funeral arrangements, picked out the casket, and paid my bills, they made my heart glad. They illustrated in living colors the word "love."

People have special talents and natural gifts. Michelle and Tosca are gifted and talented administrations. I told them what I wanted and they executed it with dedication and love. My only criteria for Steve's home going celebration was his request that people not be able to see the hollow shell of dirt he bore upon this earth, it was a temporal body of flesh. Therefore, I wanted the casket closed. I wanted God be given praise and worship for the victory of his new life in eternity. I also wanted loving pictures that displayed his joy in living. They worked out the details and made sure that everything ran smoothly.

Connie, my dearest, closest friend at the time, was battling breast cancer. Our relationship was challenged with despair and grief that fatal illnesses bring. She was devastated by Steve's death, as her love for him was so great. He was like her brother. They understood and trusted each other.

  This challenge did not stop her from giving. She gave financially anything that I needed; she even collected money in the beauty shop where we worked. Her gift to me was "giving." When her funds were depleted, she gave spiritually; she gave her love; she gave her compassion.

Connie touched a place in my heart that very few could. We both knew that we were there for each other to reach those places where human understanding alone cannot touch.

We had insight into each other's motives. At this particular time in our lives, I did not understand our relationship. It seemed as though we were being pulled apart. While this was hard for us emotionally, we immediately pushed our differences aside when my father died. It was no different when Steve died. I will never forget the comfort I found in Connie's eyes. She walked into my room and placed my head upon her shoulder saying "it's okay to cry Cheryl." I knew she understood the hurt and I didn't have to be strong with her. I cried with gut wrenching tears. I did not want to live. I did not want to face life without Steve. We were supposed to die together. We were supposed to grow old together. I felt cheated. I felt betrayed. I felt like someone was trying to pull my heart out of my chest. I screamed, but Connie would not let me go. She was not afraid of the grief, although it was heavy. She laid aside her own pain and suffering from debilitating disease and gave her shoulder, already heavy with her own pain. We held each other until we felt better. Until that moment, I could not deal with her breast cancer because I could not feel her pain. But as we held each other, we exchanged grief and cried for all the times we could not. When she left that day, I found the courage to leave my room. She gave me courage to face my fears, courage to cry, and to feel death's despair. Connie gave me permission to grieve.

Grieving may not be visible to those who see naturally. Tears of grief run beneath the surface of flesh and flows to the heart. It echoes in caves of soft screams and makes its abode in a quiet river of the past. Tears of grief then silently drop into a bottle that the Father holds.

My comfort is that He not only knows my tears, but He holds my tears. They are important to Him and He understands.

Grieving comes when we suffer loss.

God allows us to suffer loss, but He never intended for us to feel the pains of death. I believe the overwhelming pain felt from suffering loss is literally unbearable in the natural. God knows that and through the finished work of Christ, He took the sting out of death.

CHAPTER 3:
A TIME TO MOURN

Each stage of life requires wisdom to grow... Mourning is a learned process for believers. It is the part of life that challenges us to uncover our fragility. It is the reality that we are mortal...

THE HOME GOING CELEBRATION

After Connie left, I went downstairs stepping over bodies, some sleeping, some watching television, and some talking to each other. I went to the living room, my quiet place, and begin to prepare for Steve's service. I wanted his service to display the life of a victorious man of valor. I wanted the people to leave his service with a sense of hope, not despair. I wanted it to be a celebration of his triumphant entry into eternity. This would not be a funeral, and I wanted nothing of that sort. So instead of an obituary to be read silently, I thought about something to be read aloud. It was very normal for me to write love letters to Steve, so I began to write the last letter he would take into eternity with him.

A LETTER FROM YOUR WIFE

I'm sitting here, thinking of you. Your touch, your smile, your tenderness. I'm looking into your eyes. I see your insecurities, your love, and destiny. Baby, I realize I am your destiny. Each breath I breathe, each time I open my mouth I speak your words of wisdom, the words you gave me. I harvest seeds of truth planted in my heart by infallible love.

I see your heart, and though it no longer beats in the natural, my heartbeat is beating your destiny in a harmonic everlasting song of love.

Steve, your struggle not to leave me in this world alone should not have been. You thought your destiny, our future, was through. Didn't you know, YOU are my legacy. Your hopes; your dreams are my dreams, and they will be lived through your children and the many lives you have touched.

Don't look at my pain; only see my joy in being able to love you in this life as your wife. You called me your angel, but God knows you are the Angel. The angel of love, not love learned by mortal life or finite books, or even of life's so-called script; but you loved by giving -- always, always giving - not with words, but with your life.

Never again will I be touched in this life by another as yourself, only by what is left in the lives of your children, in the natural and the spiritual children you birthed and nourished. I look at these children Steve, as they whisper destiny and fulfill their purpose.

They say you were too young. They say you were just beginning to live. If they only knew your wisdom, your wisdom, your tender grace, and your rich abundant love that you sowed into broken lives. If they only knew the power of your artistic, creative touch - your tremendous musical talents. If they only knew the impact you left on so many people's lives. If they had really seen the love you gave back to the Father, they would know that death to this body is just the beginning of true life.

It's raining today and I remember how much you liked rain and storms. I remember you were always calm, peaceful, and restful. You had the key that not many people understand. You knew that without rain there is no growth. Without storms, we could not appreciate the sunshine. You knew for God's law to be fruitful it must be graced by rain.

You knew so many things in the spirit, it seemed as though you never walked in the flesh.

My hope is that I can live in your wisdom, and finish my course, and lay my life down as you did. Steve, you will be pleased to know you will always live... always live and....

Yes baby, our ministry has just begun, as you said yesterday while we were talking. But you didn't know it began when you laid your life down just as Jesus gave His life for me.

My darling, my love.

My peace, my joy.

My inspiration.

Sleep.

I love you so much.

I always will.
I always will.

Goodnight baby, Rest In Peace.

Love eternal,

Me.

,

Once I woke the later, the reality of never seeing or feeling his loving hands hit me full force and the peace of God came and flooded my mouth. I began to worship God. I didn't understand it, but that is what the peace of God does, it's surpasses understanding and takes you out the current circumstances. Oh, and I sang and cried and worshipped and cried. Peace flooded my soul.

Jesus' peace rocked me to sleep right there on that chair, my tears were my pillow, worship was my bed. It was the first time I had slept in 48 hours.

The next morning, Tosca took me to church to finish the program of Steve's service. Tyus Nedd, the youth Pastor, saw me and walk me to the door. He began to share the experience he had in losing his brother, and how his brother lived a life that most Christians would shun. He ministered to gang members and homeless people on the streets. At his funeral, the alter was filled with those people to whom he had ministered. His death touched many lives. It was then that I realize that grief was like a hand. A hand that feebly reaches out and touches the crevice of hearts that may not have much in common. It pulls the strings of the heart as instruments, making cords work together in harmony. Those cords would never be heard if they had not been touched my death.

He also spoke of how Steve had touched his life without ever spending much time together. He was intrigued by the way he lived his life and the way he loved his family.

I walked away with the comfort of knowing that my husband had touched many, many lives with his tenderness, his ability to be touched, made you feel like you were the most important thing at that time. His loving smile brightened up the hearts of many.

Suddenly, a smile came shining through my trembling tear stained face.

Later that day I had to pick out what Steve would wear. It really was important to others, but not to me. I thought, who would see it? As soon as I touched his clothes, I broke. I fell hopeless upon my face and cried. I smelled him. I felt him. He was so rea therel. I could not believe he was gone. I chose something that was special to him. He and Emaari had dressed alike on Easter in these colorful vests that Tosca made. He looks so proud wearing it. I felt it would be appropriate to place him in it. Tosca was honored and so overwhelmed that she cried.

Sunday morning came and I felt as if I wanted to run into the doors of the church. I found such a refuge in the service of the Lord, and with the people of God. It is where I feel comfortable and at home. While I was getting dressed there was something else going on in the depths of my soul. Reality was still trying to grip my senses and heart. I had to accept the fact that my husband was gone. It was like my spirit knew he was gone, but my heart, body, and mind needed more evidence.

Off we went to church. Me, Willa Mae, Mari and Debbie. (The Walker Girls). The support of my sisters made me keep my head up. I felt that they were protecting me in some strange way. I walk to the doors and was greeted by hugs and tear-filled eyes. God displayed his straight through me. It was as if I was walking out His integrity. I stood on His word. It was literal ground for me. I stood upon His promise to keep me in the perfect peace His word spoke of.

I went to my seat and looked on the stage were Steve would have been. Where was he? Why wasn't he on the stage playing his bass guitar? My son left my arms and ran towards the platform. He was looking for his daddy. He began to cry. "Where is my daddy?" he said. As my heart echoed his words, my body stood waiting for his arms to come around me in a rushed hug, then back to the stage to play for the next service. Instead it was Emaari running back to me and I hear my lips saying, "Daddy is with Jesus." As he cried on my shoulder, these words now became truth to me.

After service, I spent most of the day at the hospital with my friends, Terrisa, Roshawn and their new baby. As I looked at her eyes, I thought her life crossed "from" the threshold of eternity, as my husband "entered" into the threshold of eternity. I was overwhelmed with emotion. I held her and was given the privilege to help name her. She was gorgeous. Her name is Jhana Rae Cole.

The day of Steve's service the sky was crystal blue and the sun was shining bright. It felt like the heavens welcomed the presence of their delightful newcomer. I felt Steve smiling and his smile lit up the heavens. It was amazing how real I felt the presence of my husband from the day of his death (when I was in the hospital room with him) to the day of his home going service. He encouraged me with words like, "Stay strong Cheryl, you can do it. Trust God Cheryl." It was if he was encouraging me to make it.

The service was at 7:00 PM and the day swept by like minutes instead of hours.

All day I felt like butterflies were fluttering in my stomach. I was nervous, excited, and anxious. It was weird but I felt like a bride. I felt God's glory shining upon me. I felt chosen to uphold the name of Christ, chosen to display his glory even in tragedy.

I began to get dressed and my niece helped me. She said, "Auntie Cheryl, you look so pretty." I looked in the mirror and all I saw was me alone. Not pretty, but alone. Steve was not there and my heart was about to burst. I remember praying, "Help me, Lord. Help me through this. I cannot do it alone."

I walked down the stairs and out the door I walked with no intentions of returning, and no particular destination. I walked out of my door with the hope of walking out of this current reality into ANYWHERE else. As I turn the corner, the limousine turned the corner and snapped me back into present reality. I knew I had to go whether I wanted to or not. I took a deep breath and headed back to the house. With each step I said, "I can do all things through Christ who strengthens me. I can do all things through Christ."

When I entered the church, everyone looked so great. Everyone was in white and it seem like they were glowing. My church had never experienced death in this fashion. This was the first funeral in the sanctuary and the experience brought a sense of unity. The choir fasted and gave abundantly of their time all on behalf of my beloved. You could feel God's love as you entered the sanctuary.

There was something that I wanted to avoid... seeing the casket. I avoided it as long as I could, but the anointing was so heavy in the sanctuary that I was compelled to enter. It was an awesome casket. Gold and majestic with the look of royalty. Pictures surrounded Steve's casket of our family, depicting our lives together.

I have never felt the arms of the Lord like I did that night. He literally picked me up in place me on a cloud. I was enveloped in his love under the shadow of his wings. His shekinah glory was all over me. I was caught up in so much serenity; my feet felt as if they would not touch the ground. The joy of the Lord was overwhelming and it was contagious.

I could not really see faces. I just felt the presence of people. The church was packed to capacity and they had to turn people away. Thousands of people has come to pay honor to my husband. I was honored to be his wife.

Many people came to embrace me. Each with a story to tell, showing their sympathy. Someone even told me of a cow that had died on a farm when she was young, and how she never forgot. Another told me of her cousin's friend's mother's grandmother who died, and how devastated the family was. I really had to push back the laughter that I felt at how people viewed comfort. The ushers of the church became my bodyguards. They decided I had heard enough, and took me away until the service began.

Steve was a reserved man, not very outspoken. It was amazing the lives he had touched without words, just genuine love. Before his death, he practiced this a song with Robert, the worship leader of our church. He loved when the musicians played it instrumentally. Well, the choir wrote words to it and sang it. "Holy, my God is Holy." The beat was very up and rhythmic. "Worthy to be praised and full of glory." The choir looked down at me, singing their hearts out. I was proud to be in the family of God.

Praises rang out through the sanctuary. The atmosphere was charged full of life. My brother in-law, Theo came up and played the bass and played just like his big brother! You could almost forget this gathering was because someone died, and I was caught up in the praises of God. As a worshiper, I was drawn to the stage when my praise team sang. First, Tosca told me to come up. The rest of the team did not want to sing without me; I ran to the stage. I was emotionally full. The congregation went up in a roar. I found myself speaking. I told them that we had a reason to celebrate because the heavens were rejoicing in the homecoming of our beloved.

The men of the church had shared what Steve meant to them. My brother Johnny walked up to the platform. A complex person, his hard exterior covered the sensitive heart with me. He took a long walk to the platform and with unrehearsed words he began. "The person all of you men have been talking about is my brother. We grew up together, laughed together. You only knew him for a few years. Your acquaintance has been mostly in church. But the Steve you see in church is the same Steve you see at home. I have never seen someone so real, so true. He loved his wife, my sister, so much. I used to be jealous and envious and wondered how to love like that could be real." His voice broke, and he went down to the casket. "Steve, I know I was supposed to be the big brother, but I admire you. I look to you, and I love you, my brother. I love you." With that he took a flower from an arrangement and laid it on the closed casket, kissing the casket.

Everyone was in tears and I hurried to embrace him. Before I knew it all my family were standing there hugging, huddling in front of the casket. Behind us the congregation was on their feet, in a standing ovation for a great man, Stephen Lee Watson.

Lafayette, my pastor, preached Steve's eulogy with a twinkle in his eye. He talked about the love David had for the Lord and compared it to Steve's love for God's work. He spoke of Steve's faithfulness and commitment to the worship department. He talked directly to me, charging me to share with others the love my husband and I were privilege to have. Then he read from Habakkuk 3:19:

The Lord God is my strength, my personal bravery, and my invincible army; he makes my feet like hind's feet and will make me to walk and make progress upon my high places of trouble, suffering, or responsibility! For my chief musician; with my stringed instruments.

This passage of scripture prophetically kept me in the time of sorrow, and gave me strength for the future.

It was a night to remember in a significant way to close a chapter in my life.

THE BURIAL

It was the sixth day, Tuesday, May 2, 1994. Six days since I saw him, text him, kissed him, and unlike the day before, it was dreary and wet outside. There were no white garments for this day. I chose a black dress with leopard jewels around the neckline, one of Steve's favorite dresses.

When I came downstairs I was greeted by three women. They were mothers who have likewise experience grief. They felt that because of this joyful cloud that I had walked upon at Steve's home going service, I did not realize that Steve was dead. They felt I had not really grieved.

I looked them square in the eyes, and shared with them the reality of my loss.

"First of all, I wanted you to know that I watched my husband struggle as his heart failed and saw the agony of each labored breath. I came home that night to an empty bed. My arms ached to hold him, but they could only hold a tear soaked pillow. My children call out for him at night and wake up running into my bed for comfort, and you are asking me if I realize my husband is dead? Every place I walked in my house it echoes my husband's death. Empty rooms cry out to hear the sound of his music. Empty clothes hang in his closet. Empty plates want to hold his favorite dish. Empty stairs want to feel his feet. My heart is bleeding from the tear it has in it!

By the time I finished talking I was screaming inside, though my composure was calm. I wanted to go totally off, but I said those words calmly. God restrained me because I know what my heart felt, and it was not pretty. Needless to say, they were in tears, and apologized for interfering.

I couldn't shake the feeling of finality. This is it. I was going to bury my husband. In the ground would be his body and all that I knew of what we called life.

The cemetery was around the corner from my house, literally five minutes away. As we turn the corner to the cemetery, Steve's voice was in my ear:

"Cheryl, this is it. I can no longer go with you. I must fulfill my eternal purpose away from this life you know. God has equipped you baby. He was equipped you to live a life without me and you are going to make it. Cheryl, I wish you could see me from the eyes of the father. The latter will be greater than the former, only trust him. I wish you could see Cheryl, I wish you could see."

As I exited the car my knees felt like they were giving out. I was depleted. I do not remember who was holding me up. I believe it was my sister and my mom. I cried silent tears, feeling like half of a person, ripped into shreds, naked, violated, and stripped. I could not hear what anyone said, nor do I remember walking to the site. I only remember it being over and sitting on my bed, totally exhausted, full of sadness and despair. At the age of 34, Stephen Lee Watson was dead and gone. He was not coming back to live with me anymore. I did not know what in the world to do.

CHAPTER 4:
A TIME TO GRIEVE

Grieving is the soul's soil for change. Through precious planting, its fruit pushes a new life from the ground of sorrow...

UNCOVERING THE GRIEVING PROCESS

Immediately I was faced with mountainous decisions.

My husband had no insurance. We had just made the decision for him to go to school. He had sent me through school and patiently supported me while I build my business. I thought it was only fair to do the same for him. He wanted a career, not just a job, and I was established enough to provide while he went to trade school. He was only seven weeks off his job before he died, leaving us without any life or medical insurance.

I was financially devastated.

The church together and blessed me financially, but I needed to make a decision to leave self-employment and become an hourly laborer again. My children were two, four, and eight and we need medical insurance. Premiums were astronomical for health insurance for the self-employed. As a cosmetologist, I did not have set hours, sometimes working 12-hour days. Moreover, I needed to make a decision about where we lived. It was no longer a home to me, it was just a house. I wanted to move from that house. It held too many memories of my husband.

I felt like I was in the valley of decisions.

My husband and I were a young couple and we had made some immature financial decisions in our youth that I now faced alone. We felt we had time. I found that time is something we never possess. So, I began to make decisions one by one.

The first thing I needed to do was let go.

I am an impatient person, by nature, God hade now trust me into this new life without my permission so I felt he trusted me to bear it. However, instead of relying on Him to carry out the process, I began to do things on my own.

The first thing I did was take off my wedding rings. I took them off and put them away. I could not bear the thought of wearing them. My rings were the confirmation of covenant between my husband and I, whenever I rubber my fingers I would feel close to Steve. It was affirmation that he loved me and chose me. So, I took them off.

I never felt so loved by anyone. He cherished me and it wasn't because I was so great, because I wasn't. To the people on the outside I was popular, outgoing, self-assured, the life of the party, sweet and innocent, tiptoe through the tulips, Cheryl. But no one knew that insecure, helpless little girl inside me. No one except Steve.

He knew all those things about me and still made the decision to love and cherish me. His love was a choice no matter how insecure I was. He would say, "I am not those people who let you down Cheryl. Trust me." Each time I felt my rings, it confirmed and affirmed, "He really loves me and chose me." I believe God used Steve to deliver me from the insecurity that I bore deep inside.

When I took the rings off, I heard a sound in my inner ear. It sounded like a garment being torn, resounding the sheer agony and turmoil inside.

Understand, there is a violent stripping of your innermost being when death comes into your life.

Immediately I began to ask, "Why? What was one with my life, Lord? What did I do? What did I do to deserve this?"

Through my tears I saw a beautiful jeweled covered evening gown. It fit me perfectly, and felt good on my body. I was walking with my head up high, dancing into my destiny. All of a sudden, a hand came out of nowhere and ripped the evening gown from me, leaving me exposed and feeling violated. The other hand held a dress of sackcloth and nothing spectacular or extraordinary. In fact, it was less than ordinary and very heavy.

The voice of the hand said," Will you wear this tonight?'"

Weeping, I shook my head and thought, what was wrong with what I was wearing? It was beautiful and it fits me perfectly? What was wrong with what I was wearing?

I knew in my heart that God was speaking to me and those hands belonged to him.

God always deals with my life in vivid technicolor prophetic visions. The pictures are full of distinct color and clarity. Whenever He gives me vision, change follows.

This time was no different. The vision gave color to what I was feeling. My life was good. I had a wonderful husband, darling children, a great home, and loving friends. We loved the Lord with all our hearts, and we were full force in our ministry of worshippers. I was happy and content. Why did this tragedy come and rip my life apart?

Ignoring the latter part of my vision, I began to feel sorrow on the inside. I was not used to anyone giving to me.

I was used to giving, but not receiving. I gave money, my time, my smile and support. I would pray and encourage others. If anyone asked about my needs, I turned them away. Now, it was very hard to give my pain to anyone including...God. I allowed the pain to flow silently like waves over my heart. I cried in private, or in front of my children, or my closest friends, but not much publicly. In public I was bubbling, joyful Cheryl.

Suddenly, the phone rang and took me away from my thoughts. It was Connie. "Will you take a ride with me Cheryl? I have to go to the post office in Obetz. It should be a nice ride on such a gorgeous day."

"Sure Connie, I'll be ready." When she arrived, she looked like something was bothering her. I knew she was hurting, but there was something else behind those big bright eyes.

On the way, we talked a lot about Steve. One of her fondest memories was when we went to Chicago to her Husband's family reunion. We sat on the hill watching fireworks debating heavily about the Bible. Connie's husband, Darrell and I were going at it with his brothers. Steve and Connie were calm, retreating from the debate, they played with the kids, shaking their heads at us. "There they go again" they laughed saying, "This may be a long one." Connie enjoyed Steve's peaceful presence- it relaxed her. She felt he was a perfect balance to my outgoing rambunctious personality.

Connie had a lot in common with Steve in her voice broke as she talked. "Cheryl, I know you miss him girl, but you must trust the Lord. He has something great in store for you. Steve is with Jesus."

Ironically, when she said those words, I heard a still voice in my head saying, "Connie is not going to be with you much longer. I knew the cancer was progressing, but I did not know what "much longer" meant, a year, a month, a week? What are you doing God? Why are you doing this to me?

We spent the rest of the day just sharing thoughts about life and our future. Suddenly, I felt overwhelmed and closed in.

"Will you take me home Connie?"

"Are you all right?" she said.

"Yes, I'm just fine," I lied. She hugged me and took me home.

That evening I felt very heavy, overloaded with grief and despair. Oh God, will this ever end? Will you take this load away for me? There was no answer.

Heaven was silent.

Connie's life, though short-lived, was very influential to those around her and especially to those who loved her. She was totally submitted to the Lord. She reminded me of a masterpiece that God created in the likeness of Queen Esther of biblical times.

I remembered a vision Connie had. She was at the throne of God. The Father held out his scepter to her, granting permission to enter into His presence. In October of the same year, Connie went to see the King.

ASHES TO BEAUTY

The hardest part to write about is the process of grieving, the phase of letting go, saying goodbye to past reality. A part of you yells "I'm not ready to let go." Places that we shared, songs we heard, fears we conquered, tears we cried. All those things that make a life real are now memories slowly fading into vapors.

Wisdom has taught me that life goes on. You learn to laugh again and really feel it, instead of the nagging numbness of yesterday's laughter. You cry, but not so much about the past or the memories, but about the new life that have no image of your loved ones, only shadows.

The scripture quoted by David was "Yea though I walk through the valley of the shadow of death…" Valleys are placed that join land together. Valleys are places that rebuild integrity. They are places of growth, places that are inevitable if you are walking with the Lord.

Valleys are often found near bodies of water.

In the beginning stages of grief, you feel you are in a sea riding waves, and balancing on the water. Only soon to be overcome and overwhelmed by the strength of the turbulent waves that wash you back to land, depleted and weak. The waves of pain hit you at anytime and anyplace, and can become a hindrance if you don't move out the way of its violent crash.

You must not visit the past so much, but look at the present and to the future in order to keep your head above the water of circumstance.

After the waves come valleys, the low places, the empty places, the character building places where you make a conscious effort to move on with your life. You then begin desire something new, like furniture, a car, or a house it's your "salute" to a beginning again. The valley is the place of reality. The place of coming to terms with death of the past, bringing the experience to the present.

Valleys are usually followed by mountains. Mountains are places where strength is renewed, victory is gained, it is a triumphant place. Although you are still grieving, and climbing is fierce, you gain strength in the climb. Your faith is stretched, your hinds' feet are strengthened and you victoriously climb... only to find out when you reach the top, God will require a sacrifice.

We, as Christians try to avoid mountains and base our New Testament beliefs on the power of moving mountains. However, I am not talking about telling your problems or circumstance that hinders your growth to move out of the way. I am talking about the inevitable journey of submitted lives that answer the call of the mountains as Abraham did in order to sacrifice his promise, his only son, at Mount Moriah. Jesus also answered the call when He climbed Golgotha's hill and became the perfect sacrifice.

When we leave the valley, we climb mountains, thereby engaging in the process of growth and life.

Did you know that you cannot climb a mountain looking down? You must look upward, forgetting those things that are behind you and reach for those things which ahead, pressing towards the high call of the mountain where we, like Jesus, become the sacrifice laid upon the altar, burnt beyond recognition and transformed into ashes. What becomes apparent is a visible manifestation that what you were is not who you are.

"Lord I build an altar, and there I lay my will the sacrifice is me, oh Lord, and there I yield and there I'll stay until you have your way in me.

I'll be just like you.
I'll be tried and true.
I will have a pure heart.
I'll be just like you.
Mold me and make me in Your image Lord.
I'll surrender all.

I'll obey your call.
I lay at the alter Lord.

Songs like this carried me from riding waves to climbing mountains. I finally cried, "I want to live at the top of the mountain." I laid down my life as Steve's wife and went down to the valley, only to find out that I had to lay the blessed consummation of our marriage on the altar.

You see, the intimacy of lovemaking brought peace and security to my being. I felt safe, loved and needed as I have fulfilled the desires of my husband, and as he answered the needs of my body with the tenderness, my body and soul was satisfied, fulfilled.

One morning I dreamt about Steve. His corpse laid in my bed. The dream made the corpse appear as a normal part of my life. It laid in my bed and was never buried in the ground.

The corpse came alive and called for me, I became angry and would not come. Though others were happy for the resurrection of my husband's corpse, I was not. I was afraid. Afraid that it was only a dream and I would wake up disappointed. Finally, resigning all my fears I went to the room where he was and he held me in the way that only Steve could hold me. A volcano of emotion erupted within my being, emotions that had lay brewing in the center of my being, bubbled over. "Oh, Steve," I cried. "I can't do this. It hurts so bad. I haven't been able to FEEL love since you left."

When I woke from the dream, tears flowed inside me. I realize that it was the precious Holy Spirit coming in his gentle but subtle way. Coming in my dreams, teaching me who I was, urging me to let go....

The dream let me know I was still holding on to the sanctity of my marriage vow, to love Steve only. Though I would like to take the credit for keeping my body saved, set apart and celibate waiting for my new husband, I can't. The real reason for celibacy was unresolved grief holding me to the security of my marriage vows.

The Holy Spirit said, "remember till death parts us."

My soul interpreted these words and hid me from the truth. Keep my vows alive…but… Death had parted us.

Vows or promises are not broken when they are sealed with faith and the determination. The hardest part in the grieving process is understanding that death destroys or abolishes the wedding vows or any promises made.

Widowed men marry quickly to cope with the hurt of death's destruction. Widowed women never marry to cope with the pain. Neither person allows the vow to fall to the ground and die, to shatter its purpose into the soil and bring new life.

It seems we sometimes hate the law of life - that seed must fall to fertile ground and die to produce life. Thus, we become stuck in the death process, never experiencing the blessed new life.

So, I went to the altar again to repeat my vows. This time I took them to God, so they could be consumed, for our God is consuming fire.

…. I surrender all, I'll obey your call, I lay at the altar Lord.

Finding myself at the altar helped me look at the vision of the evening gown in a new light. I had presented myself to God as a living sacrifice.

Presenting myself to God meant I gave myself as a present to God. We are excited when gifts are presented to us, and we rip the gift-wrap off of the package to see what's inside.

God did that. He was excited about the gift I gave Him and He ripped off the blue sequined gown to reveal what was inside.

Now that I have returned to the altar, my motives and will are altered. My whole being is altered. The surrender of things old, though dear, has become ashes at the altar. Now the smoke of my ashes fills the nostrils of God and He sweetly breathes His beautiful life into my transformed being.

CHAPTER 5: A TIME TO HEAL

While writing this book, I realized some truths that sustain my life. These small stones of truth carry me through difficult times of healing.

MIRROR MIRROR

I was feeling the aftermath of what I call my "waves" of grief when my brother David came by to visit me. He asked me how I was doing. Steve and David were best friends and until that time we had not spoken in detail of Steve's death.

We were talking about dating again and excepting the "new me" as an unmarried woman. He advised that I should take my time, saying "Cheryl, you have a whole life before you. You are young and full of life. Don't allow anyone to dictate to you their own fears or expectations. Be true to yourself, and as long as you can look in this mirror and not turn away from its reflection, you are okay. When you can't look at yourself anymore, will you look in the mirror and turn away from what you see, then that's when you need to make adjustments in your life".

He probably does not know the impact those words had on my life. The wisdom of those words holds a richness that cannot be purchased. When coping with tragedy you will encounter many people who have expectations of what you should be doing. They make comments like; "it's been a year, now you can go on with your life." Or some will say, "you'll never get over such a tragedy, so don't even try."

Their words sought to keep me in the past or propel me into the future, but when I walk to the tempo of the mirror and looked into the reflection of Christ, my direction was clear. His time became my time, and His timing is always perfect.

I look into the mirror often to keep my life in check, making sure I'm not hiding from its reflection, too ashamed of what I see. It helps me remain focused and real.

A QUEST FOR PEACE

Romans 5:11 became one of my favorite scriptures in my process of grief and my quest to find peace. I realized in order to have peace with God you must be justified by faith.

Being justified by faith allows your mind to be covered with the righteousness of God, and brought under the subjection of Christ. How can you find justice in a work of God that seems to make no sense, that seems so unreal, so unjust?

My husband and I were devout Christians. My children were all under the age of nine. He was only 34 years old and in right standing with God, his family, and the people of God. By his physician's standard, Steve was healthy. There was absolutely no reason for him to die!

I found that God's justice is not predicted upon our social status. It has nothing to do with our standards of living. Moreover, it is definitely not based on our emotions or on our way of thinking.

God's justice is based solely upon his ability to be God. He has knowledge of the full picture, instead of freeze frames of our life. He has authority to create all in on all.

Psalms 24th chapter says, "the earth is the Lords and the fullness thereof, the world and they that dwell therein." This includes everything and excludes nothing. God has the sovereign ability to see beyond our limited vision. He has infinite ability to appropriate grace beyond the pains of grief. His awesome wisdom makes the right decision amidst our temporal adversity. God knows... we do not understand with our limited ability to comprehend; therefore, we need faith.

Faith is not predictable upon what we see, touch, feel, or smell. Faith takes the invisible wisdom of our God and rocks us in His everlasting arms. He's the all-knowing, all-wise Father who holds us with the same arms that he holds the universe. He measures the waters of the earth in the hollow of His hand. He is our peace and our very righteousness.

Proclaiming to God that He is right releases the pressures of making it right. It releases the guilt of not being able to change circumstances and position you in the place to receive direction from God. This is one of the hardest areas of trust in my life. Sometimes I fight against the provision of God and fall back into the bottomless pit of whys and concerns. However, His peace surpasses my limited understanding, envelops my life, picks me up and returns me to right standing with God.

I'M DREAMING...

Sometimes in my dreams you appear with big smiles and twinkling eyes. I realize you are not really here, it is just temporary. Yet my heart still leaps and caresses the image of you in my life. I shut my eyes tight praying not to awaken, wanting to stay there with you as long as I can. I take in every detail of your appearance to complete my memory of you so they are accurate consuming your actions affirming, yes that's how you would respond... and I embrace you holding on to your image as it slowly disappears...

Then I realize you are only a dream and my eyes are open wide. Reality hits. I am drained by the visit with you. My emotions pierced with a deep sigh, feeling the disappointment like a broken engagement. My heart beats as it falls from a high place of you to the low crevice where you remain somewhere deep inside...

A very real part of the healing process is dreaming. It's your minds way of coping with reality. Dreaming allows you to visit places you may never have the chance to visit, do things you would never do. Dreaming gives you back precious memories of the subconscious that reality would not allow you to penetrate. It is temporary, waiting for you to wake, it fulfills a purpose in the line of grieving process.

As you walk in the reality of death, you are faced with painful memories. Sometimes through visions, sometimes through dreams. Those places grip your heart and leave you with a pain that is indescribable. It's like a knife in your heart. It can leave you bitter, angry, hopeless and in despair. The questions become a loud echo in the pit of your being that crescendos into an audible sound upon your lips. Why did you have to go? Why did you have to leave this life? In those times, it is very hard to focus on the present or future, for this time captures you and attempts to keep you in the past. It arrests all trodden steps and makes you feel you haven't taken any steps in the direction of recovery.

I learned not to dwell upon the dreams or share it, but rather, I would cry until I felt better. The reality is that the departed love is gone and will not return to this life as we know it. Now I know we will see them again, but not with earthly purpose. We will recognize who they are but we will all be unveiled. Our true identity of the Father will reflect in each other's life, forgetting the mortal pains and joy in our journey to the eternal and embrace the triumph of a found destiny in the everlasting. Now that is hope! I can rejoice that when I meet my loved ones again, we'll see the transformed and they will see the immortal.

RECOVERY

CPR- Cleansing, Purging, Reforming for Change, Perfection and Refinement

I would be lying to you if I said that the road of recovery or life after death of a loved one is a sweet walk through the park. There are issues the natural man goes through as well as strongholds that need to be addressed.

The accuser of the brethren always sends guilt into a broken life. I always thought to myself, maybe if I had started CPR earlier Steve would still be alive. Or maybe if I had led a more healthier life, he would have had a better chance of living. Or, maybe if we didn't have such a busy life. Maybe. Maybe. Maybe. My mind felt heavy, like it was in a tight squeeze.

I was expressing the guilty feelings to my friend Gary and he came up with the acronym; CPR cleansing, purging, reforming for change, perfection, and refinement. Gary recommended that instead of carrying guilt, that I should look at what God has done for me. God used this tragedy to change my direction, to perfect my walk, and find my purpose, but first I had to let him cleans my guilt, purge my motive, then reform my way of thinking.

Those words loosed in the prongs of guilt from around my mind. I had to get the mind of God and his thoughts to receive healing. I realized that I had issues concerning grief. His purging brought out the feelings that were covered from the depths of my soul. I was uncovered. I was unveiled in God and began to show me myself. Instead of hiding, I allowed his grace to cover me and strengthen me. Though unveiled, my direction was clear.

UNVEILED

I began to remember things that had been tucked deep inside. Simple things that had profound meanings. Memories like how Steve would lift me into his arms and twirl me around, tossing all my cares and cautions to the

wind. He twirled me in the park when he proposed to me. He twirled me on our wedding day as he stole a kiss on the side of the church. He twirled me on the platform of the church when I surprised him with an early arrival from an out of town trip. He twirled me on his return from a men's retreat. On one knee, he affirmed his love as he kissed my hand. The twirl of my mind spun when he said, "You are my queen, Cheryl Denise, and I am God's servant. He is the King." Those twirls always gave me security that he had control. Control enough to keep me in a spin, dizzy from his love.

While reflecting upon that security, God gave me vision and of myself twirling in a flower covered garden. This time I was alone and the twirl became a dance. Then the Father God picked me up and twirled me in His arms, showing me the security of His love. He covered me in that time of utter aloneness.

The uncovering began. A total change in my being, I was no longer in the arms of my security. My arms long to wrap around him. I'd watch the door hoping and expecting him to return. Every time the phone rang I would answer in anticipation of hearing his sweet voice. I would play the answering machine of his message over and over just to feel he was near. Many nights I would sob and weep. The pain in my heart grasped my breath, gripped my mind, and swallowed me.

One night I found myself crawling on the floor trying to find some air, some kind of relief from the grief that seem to overtake and smother me with each wave of agony. In deep waters of grief, I felt as if I would drown.

"God!", I would cry, "I can't bear this! Please take me. Why don't you take us all?"

Then I heard the voice of God saying, "give it to me. I could bear it. You cannot bear this grief. I bore it for you. Please give it to me. GIVE ME YOUR PAIN!"

When the enemy comes in, like a flood God will raise up a standard. In other words, He will give you a solid place to stand. He will give you His truth to hold on to and when you feel the bottom has fallen out from under you he will give you a word to stand upon.

I realized that the enemy would have loved to see me drown in my sorrow. God took me that night above the waves of sorrow as I gave Him my heart. God lifted me above the waves of sorrow as I gave him my truth. God loves truth. It is the reality of His very character. I told Him I could not bear the pain. I told him He made a mistake. He held me and said, "I'll take it." I beat him with fists of anger and hurt. "He said, I'll take it." He became a strong tower where I found safety at night. He became my security. Now when faced with issues, I give God the truth of what I'm feeling. He gives my His strength, His character, and His love.

LONELY OR EMPTY

I was alone. My spirit man understood immediately and became stronger day by day. However, my soul or emotions were always a step behind. As my soul caught up with the reality my spirit has already obtained, I realize there is a distinct difference between being lonely and being empty.

Many days, (especially holidays or sunny days), I was faced with being alone. Not from the presence of someone because I have three children, but the ability of relating to someone, to have someone understand and care for and tend for me. I wanted to be with someone I could relate to.

So, I would tell the Father, "I am lonely" and I would not get a response. I would cry and ask Him to just let the phone ring, just let somebody come by.

God finally said to me, "You are not alone." "Then what is this feeling? I just need a tangible something to touch and feel. I feel so alone. I'm literally starving for attention."

Then...a light came into my mind.

I was starving from the loss of my husband, and the lack of attention he once gave me. I was empty. Not full. Not satisfied. Empty. Spent. Deflated.

The difference between being alone and empty is the feelings and emotions experience in dealing with them both.

Alone isolates you. It is a feeling of abandonment or being deserted.

Emptiness is the feeling of hunger, thirst, weakness, or desperation. Empty makes you hungry to feel someone's arms around you or to hear someone speak to you. Hungry to feel special, to belong. Then you feel depleted, deflated, or not even wanting to fight, always sighing breaths of tiredness or weariness.

Both are feelings that must be dealt with in the presence of God. The word of God declares that in his presence is the fullness of joy. The joy of the Lord (literally fills you UP) and becomes your strength.

The word also says, Therefore, with joy shall you draw waters from the well of salvation. These three scriptures became my bread and water in my lonely, empty times.

Like David, I began to thirst for the presence of God, to pant as a deer after water. For in the water, I found strength in the time of wariness in refuge in the time of trouble. God filled the void in my life through worship and praise, and I became lost in my need for Him. I found that my passion became compassion and my sympathy became empathy, because now I was identified with the fellowship of His sufferings.

THE PROCESS OF BECOMING ONE

There is a unique process that comes with the endurance of loss and grief. That is the process of becoming one again – single, whole, and by yourself. You learn how to stand alone. As a single woman who was once married, there are certain issues that you must address.

As a married woman, my actions were covered by my spouse. The vision for my future and our household was shared. My husband held the vision in his head and his actions he walked out the vision. As his wife, I upheld his vision and helped him meet what God purposed for our lives together.

Learning about my body again and learning how to bring it under subjection of the will of Christ was a very frustrating process. My body had sung to the harmonious lyrics of my husband and was awakened to His love in true covenant. My body had once held the covenant of the marriage bed. It was something that brought me great pleasure, giving me the opportunity to learn the power of touch and the expression of body language.

I had learned to speak with my body and love my husband by God's Gift of covenant of making love. I came into the knowledge of the importance of covenant. In marriage, we chose each other, by affirming the choice to love each other we affirm the covenant of marriage.

When you suffer loss of a husband and return to singleness, you are now covered by God the Father- El Shaddai. You belong to him. He now covers you with His grace and infuses purpose and NEW vision.

This was an awesome responsibility. God trusted me with the process of becoming one in Him, through Him. I am all one as a single, whole person. I now find clarity and have single vision, and my covering is the Lord God Most High.

Earlier in the throes of grief, I didn't know how to carry to the new vision. I didn't realize God as my covering, and confused the death of my spouse with being exposed.

But by changing my perspective of being single again, I experienced the opportunity for God to reveal Himself to me. I became naked, pure, uncovered, and not holding back. I learned to cast down imaginations or images that were exalted against the knowledge of Christ. I am now complete in Christ and open for the new He will send my way. Now I am free and WHOLE. (ALL ONE)

There are many new things I has to open myself up to and it brought closure to what was. Old things had to pass away.

PRESENT DESIRES HELP DISSIPATE PAST PAINS....

As a single woman, I found myself always BUSY. That way I would forget the pain of my loss and block thoughts that would come to depress me. There was also a need to find myself and stay open to new things. During that time, I found a truth that I hold presently: Present desires help dissipate past pains.

I indulged myself into reading and writing, and I had an insatiable thirst for God's word. I studied not just for knowledge, but I really wanted to know Him.my desire was towards God and my heart panted after his word. My desire was so intense, I did not have time to massage the hurt of the past.

The more I desired, the more I thirsted, the more He would fill me with His love. His presence encompassed, overwhelmed me. I was alive full of hope and vigor. Although the past was very real and painful, my present desire for God became my strength and my song.

Little by little I no longer saw a dark empty future. The Son of righteousness shined His purpose upon me and my desire was toward Him. I began the process of letting go of what was, and looking forward to the future. I was no longer Stephen Watson's wife. I was a single woman. My life began to take a new direction. My walk, my way of thinking, my job and my friends changed.

FINDING FRIENDS

In the process of change, God strategically placed people in my life. The first single friend found me through assignment of the Holy Spirit. We instantly connected in the spirit, although we were two different individuals. She was quiet, I am not. She was conservative, I am not. God made us accountable to each other to strengthen each other, to uphold each other. Through friendship and compassion, I have conquered many hurdles and released the anxiety of being unmarried with children, and the tension that comes in the season of singleness. Vickie came to me with empty hands. She was curious about the strength God had given me, but internally she didn't come to take, but rather to give. She did not realize that the assignment given by God, was not only to strengthen me, but to restore her ability to trust in the human spirit through God's grace. He allowed me to fill her empty hands with genuine friendship and though relationships are tried, what remains after the fire is always precious. I'll never forget her.

Relationships played an important part in my healing process. Filling my life with new relationships helped me cherish and appreciate old ones. It opened my heart and broadened my perspective of God's creation. It helped ease the pains of the past and once again I was thirsty for life. I wanted to live.

I have bumped into many people. Curious people wondering if I would make it, puzzled people, wondering how I made it, and people intrigued of who I am becoming. Many people have not had the courage to ask me questions or reach down inside my painful places of grief, until I encountered someone who I call my "little sister."

She came to me in her insecurities, wrapped in a very hard shell of mistrust and asked, "would you mentor me, and keep me in mind if I act up?" My first response to this very stout, athletic, very outspoken, just downright big young lady was, "why do you need someone to look after you, you should be looking after me?"

But there was something genuine about her. Behind the eyes of all this bigness, twinkled a very awkward and hurt, misunderstood little girl. She was the ever so professional, ever so conservative, ever so serious Doreen. Yet underneath all those titles, her smile was genuine.

I have counseled many individuals throughout my ministry, pulling down many strongholds under the guidance of the Holy Spirit, but never had someone asked Cheryl, "Whose shoulder do you cry on?" Who do you lean on when you're weak? When did you have time to grieve the loss of your father, or Connie? But Doreen did.

Somehow, she touched that painful grief I had held onto regarding Connie. And I cried over guilt. I cried not being the best friend I should have been. I cried over our lost relationship. Doreen told me things about Connie's feelings that I never understood. She shared how Connie wanted to shield me from the pain of her disease, and was shunning me away to protect me. Sometimes Doreen never said a word, just lent me one of her big shoulders to sob on, or she would say "Do you need a hug?" Wait a minute! I'm supposed to be the mentor.

In one of our many conversations about Connie and Steve, she asked if she reminded me of Connie. I replied, "I don't know. "I never really thought about it." Doreen, in her honest way, shared, "I was just wondering because I could never measure up to Connie's friendship. And although I'm very competitive, I cannot compete with the dead."

Those words, though very simple, had an enormous truth to them. Sometimes missing a loved one places you in a fantasy world where you place the expectations of past relationships upon new ones. This causes the loved one around you to be frustrated, helpless, and drains their very own precious character from them. We must be careful not to live in the memories of our past relationships, placing demands on our new friends that will never measure up. Not allowing the expression of their own uniqueness touch our lives and add new chapters to pages of destiny, not trodden.

Memories of loved ones are very significant. It gives color to the full picture of life. But living inside of this memory keeps you in in unrealistic world of hopelessness of the things that have no life, becoming baggage and heavy grief that we cannot bear. I now make a conscious effort not to put such a load on my loved ones.

Although I have been through an incredible amount of change in my life since the tragedies are suffering, somethings were unshakable. When my life felt as though it was a big whirl, I enjoyed the calmness and gentle care of my friend Tosca. She was always giving me support, even when she didn't exactly know how. We became friends when I was a married woman, and our families became inseparable. Steve's tragic death brought a load of grief into our relationship and we found ourselves with a true challenge. How could we except each other now that I was single? Our conversations and schedule required change. Likewise, our time together changed. We were like strangers, yet too close to notice the impact this tragedy placed on our friendship.

All Tosca wanted was her friend to be OK, happy again. All I wanted was my life back, to feel normal again and her husband Gary vowed to my husband to take care of me and keep all prospective men or "wolves" as he called him away from the children and I. We didn't know how to make it all work, we didn't know how to adjust to the new ME.

In our struggle to find each other in this new life, we held onto the love that true friendship brings. Dissolving the friendship was out of the question- we had invested too much, and we have been through too much together. Even though we felt the friendship dangling by a thread, we held on. So, we adjusted. We adjusted our walk, our talk, and the way we viewed each other. We let go of what we had in the past and open up to what God has prepared for us. The respect, trust, love and concern we had for each other was only strengthened and became deeper through crying, yelling and being transparent with one another. Now, our friendship cannot be duplicated, and we will end our lives together as friends.

I believe while grieving, friends or brought alongside you to keep you grounded, to keep your sanity, to challenge you and support your new life. It's hard to become whole and healed when you don't have the support of someone who knew you before, someone who knew you after, and someone who only knows the you, you are becoming. It is a completeness that brings your life full circle, full and complete.

You need people who can laugh at the past, cry in the present pain and push you into the new, all at the same time. My friends have done that and I don't know where I would be without them.

My family's support has literally been my stability. There is nothing that keeps you real like your family. Frequently they would say, "I know this is a bad day for you, but you got to pay your phone bill and feed the kids. Go to work!" Or my mom would say, "Child, how you doing? and before I could answer she would tell me how she was feeling or what she needed, making my heart warm just knowing I was needed.

Life goes on. There are problems to face, new hurtles to climb, new fears to conquer and pain to bear. But as a wise old mother of my church would say, "I wouldn't trade nothing for my journey." I never thought I'd be using that old southern dialect, but those words have meaning.

STRENGTH TO LIVE

Once I grasped the reality that God's purpose for me was to live not as I was, but as a new being, I began to apply his grace to my life, walk in HIS justice of God and accept his decision for my life.

Once I changed my way of thinking by seeing God's provision, integrity, and will for my life, then God was able to reveal His purpose for the season I was in.

"God, your decision to take my husband was right and your judgements are pure," were the hardest words ever to escape my mouth. I found myself saying those words while laying before the Lord, crying out for His direction and His mercy.

His reply was, "I am the Lord your God the Just One, the Sovereign and Reigning King! And I have called you into the Kingdom for such a time as this!"

I realize that grace is never insufficient. I didn't have to beg for his mercy. He was reigning King, allowing me to enter into the court of the Most High. He had extended Hs scepter to me, and to reign in His courts meant I must also suffer in this life to experience His resurrection power.

There must be a breaking of your Will so the costly anointing can flow out of your brokenness. Brokenness opens the pathway for the river of resurrection power to flow. It opens your eyes to purpose and destiny and into a whole new world in the Christ life.

The alabaster box of your will must be broken in the costly oil must anoint the feet of purpose so destiny can be fulfilled.

I don't know the reason I endured the tragedy I faced in 1994. All I know is my life has become fuller. Trees outside my windows seem to have more color than they used to. The smile of a loved one is worth more than gold. Tears grip my heart like never before. My children's laughter rings like a bell in my ears and I'm alive.

Does tragedy have to come to change a life?

No, I don't believe that.

I do believe that surrender in death to the flesh comes from the pain of suffering in obedience to the sovereignty of God.

In His omniscience, He is wise enough to see the full picture, past frames and dark strokes of tragedy, suffering and pains, to paint our eternal immortal lives.

Solomon in all his wisdom said in Ecclesiastes, *"To everything there is a season and a time to every purpose under the heaven." In a few scriptures, he covered the span of life from birth to death.* Finally, in Chapter 3, verse 11, Solomon says, *"He hath made everything beautiful in His time."*

This is my benediction to the OLD as I pay homage to my New!

Now unto Him who has the ability to make all things beautiful. To take precious ashes and give it a new life called beauty. To Him who finds pleasure in the death of His saints and pleasure to bruise His son. To Him whose had hung the sun, moon, and stars once, and now they hand still. To Him who causes the trees to bend their leaves to Him in praise in the midst of a turbulent storm, and allow the softness of the wind to mysteriously breathe upon lives. To His wisdom to clothe His creation with garments in every season. Unto him that mercies line up at dawn to drop upon us live dew. To the powerful, all wise, all knowing, all caring keeper of my soul... Do I lift up this garment of life. My pleasure, my King, what a blessed opportunity to wear Your love from your gracious Almighty closet.

I will forever praise You and give You honor, majesty and dominion.

MY LIFE HAS CHANGED MY LORD, I LOVE YOU!

PROLOGUE

As a personal friend and brother in Christ, I've seen Cheryl Watson (Singletary) accept willingly a transformation that would have otherwise taken many under. I've had to stand by, in what seemed to me a helpless manner, and watch God take her from one level of glory to the next. Often when we think of change, we remind ourselves of the end result and rarely take into account the process that must unfold to get us there. Having the God ordained honor to be a part of the life and times of this woman of God has indeed been a resounding joy.

As God speaks constantly from eternity, His voice reverberates the earth seeking whom He can find to echo in the earth what is being spoken from heaven. God has a myriad of qualified vessels from which to choose at any given moment in time. God has chosen one of his prized treasures in Watson, a gifted and anointed writer. CHERYL possesses the unique ability to capture God's word in her heart, while at the same time translating God's word in a clear, concise, reality based manner. I can only marvel as this writer so prolifically shares her most inward being in total transparency. I realize that in order to release such a sweet fragrance in the earth, God had to obtain the breaking of the alabaster box from heaven.

In this, her first book, the pages of "The Widow's Garment" are much more than a mere testimonial. Cheryl has lived every bittersweet page and has allowed God's definition of her to reign gloriously in her life.

Those who seem broken beyond repair, those who feel abandoned by God but afraid to say it, and those who do not believe they have the courage and faith to live again, this book is for you! This book will not only challenge believers in their faith toward God, but it will equally propel them to unprecedented heights and depths in the relationships that God has placed in their lives.

Apostle Gary Smith

Over the years, I watched as this writer grew and bloomed into a wonderful mother, sister, and influential person within our ministry. As you read this book, I hope and pray that you not merely read words typed on a page, but that you also feel the heart behind the words.

Cheryl has given her whole heart and the transparency of her experience allows you, the reader, to journey with her. Therefore, as you walk through your own personal journey, these pages reveal and give you access to the keys that can open doors to your destiny.

My final words are to the writer: Cheryl, a diamond finds itself hidden in the earth until the exact hour, minute, and second it is to be uncovered to the world. Once exposed, the true value of the stone is also revealed. This is your hour of coming forth. It is the display to the world of not only the glory of God that is in your life, but most of all the glory that is working through your life.

Pastor Tyus Nedd

www.ingramcontent.com/pod-product-compliance
Lightning Source LLC
Chambersburg PA
CBHW070104100426
42743CB00012B/2647